D0786484

...RIDGEVIEW LIBRARY DISTRICT

GERONIMO

BY SANTANA HUNT

Gareth Stevens
PUBLISHING

Please visit our website, www.garethstevens.com. For a free color catalog of all our high-quality books, call toll free 1-800-542-2595 or fax 1-877-542-2596.

Library of Congress Cataloging-in-Publication Data

Hunt, Santana.
  Geronimo / Santana Hunt.
      pages cm. — (Native American heroes)
  Includes bibliographical references and index.
  ISBN 978-1-4824-2685-4 (pbk.)
  ISBN 978-1-4824-2686-1 (6 pack)
  ISBN 978-1-4824-2687-8 (library binding)
  1. Geronimo, 1829-1909—Juvenile literature. 2. Apache Indians—Kings and rulers—Biography—Juvenile literature. 3. Apache Indians—Wars—Juvenile literature. I. Title.
  E99.A6H86 2015
  979'.004972—dc23
  [B]
                                                   2014048106

Published in 2016 by
Gareth Stevens Publishing
111 East 14th Street, Suite 349
New York, NY 10003

Copyright © 2016 Gareth Stevens Publishing

Designer: Laura Bowen
Editor: Kristen Rajczak

Photo credits: Cover, p. 1 Transcendental Graphics/Getty Images; cover, pp. 1–24 (series art) Binkski/Shutterstock.com; p. 5 Frank A. Rinehart/Wikimedia Commons; pp. 7, 15 blinkblink/Shutterstock.com; p. 9 G. Dagli Orti/DEA/Getty Images; p. 11 Ben Wittick/Wikimedia Commons; p. 13 FPG/Getty Images; p. 17 Camillus S. Fly/Getty Images; p. 19 Photo Quest/Getty Images; p. 21 Apic/Getty Images.

All rights reserved. No part of this book may be reproduced in any form without permission in writing from the publisher, except by a reviewer.

Printed in the United States of America

CPSIA compliance information: Batch #CS15GS: For further information contact Gareth Stevens, New York, New York at 1-800-542-2595.

CONTENTS

Boldface words appear in the glossary.

Apache Leader

Geronimo was a great leader of the Apache people. He fought for Apache freedom and their right to live on their homeland. Though he was forced to **surrender**, Geronimo remains a Native American hero.

5

In 1829, Geronimo was born with the name Goyathlay in present-day Arizona. "Goyathlay" means "one who yawns." He was part of the Chiricahua Apache tribe. They lived on land owned by Mexico at the time.

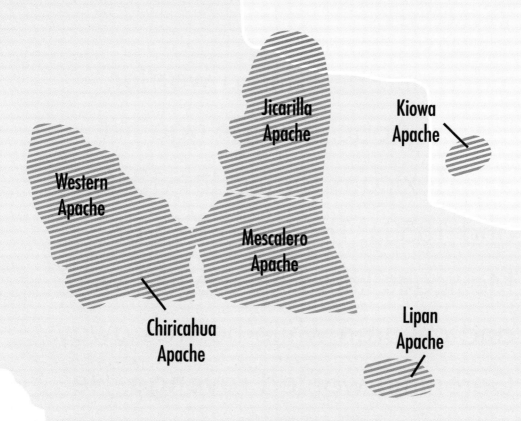

US TERRITORY, 1830

Kiowa
Apache

Jicarilla
Apache

Western
Apache

Mescalero
Apache

Chiricahua
Apache

Lipan
Apache

MEXICO

7

Warrior

Geromino became a warrior. He led Apache **raids** against the Mexicans during the 1840s and 1850s. Then, a group of Mexicans killed his mother, wife, and children while he was away. Geronimo wanted **revenge**. He fought against the Mexicans even more **fiercely**.

Geronimo became a leader among his people and known for his strength in battle. He was so feared, the Mexican soldiers fighting him called on St. Jerome for help. He took on the name Geronimo, Spanish for Jerome, because of it.

Settlers Arrive

After war with Mexico, the United States gained lands that included the Apache homelands. By the 1870s, the US government was moving Native American groups onto **reservations**. Settlers began moving west and taking over the Apache territory.

In 1872, Geronimo and his people were moved to a reservation that was partly on their old lands. They were unhappy. When they were moved to another reservation with other Apache 2 years later, Geronimo's people became even angrier.

Nevada

Utah
Territory

Colorado
Territory

UNITED STATES, 1872

California

Arizona
Territory

New Mexico
Territory

Apache
Reservations,
1870s

Pacific
Ocean

MEXICO

Escape!

Geronimo felt the reservation was a **prison**. He led raids off the reservation and often had to be brought back by the US Army. This went on for about 10 years! Geronimo's final surrender occurred near the Mexican border in 1886.

Exile

Geronimo and his followers were sent to Florida in **exile**. They spent time doing very hard work there, as well as in Alabama and Oklahoma. The exile only increased Geronimo's fame among his people. They thought he was brave and honorable.

19

Nationally Known

Geronimo wasn't able to reclaim the Apache's territory. However, he became well known enough to take part in national events, such as the parade celebrating Theodore Roosevelt winning the presidency. His story lives on in a book, *Geronimo: His Own Story*.

THE LIFE OF GERONIMO

1829 ○ Geronimo is born.

1850 ○ Geronimo's mother, wife, and children are killed.

1870s ○ Native Americans are moved to reservations across the United States

1886 ○ Geronimo surrenders to US troops. He is exiled to Florida.

1894 ○ Geronimo moves to a reservation in Oklahoma.

1909 ○ Geronimo dies.

GLOSSARY

exile: the state of forced absence from one's home

fiercely: in an excited manner

prison: a place of captivity, commonly for those who break the law

raid: a sudden attack

reservation: land set aside by the US government for Native Americans

revenge: to harm someone in return for harm done

surrender: to give up

FOR MORE INFORMATION

BOOKS

Beck, Ari, and Carolyn Dunn. *Coyote Speaks: Wonders of the Native American World.* New York, NY: Abrams Books for Young Readers, 2008.

Spilsbury, Richard. *Geronimo.* Chicago, IL: Raintree, 2014.

WEBSITES

Geronimo
www.indians.org/welker/geronimo.htm
Read about Geronimo's life and some famous quotes of his.

Native Americans: Apache Peoples
www.ducksters.com/history/native_american_apache.php
Learn more about the Apache people and Geronimo here.

Publisher's note to educators and parents: Our editors have carefully reviewed these websites to ensure that they are suitable for students. Many websites change frequently, however, and we cannot guarantee that a site's future contents will continue to meet our high standards of quality and educational value. Be advised that students should be closely supervised whenever they access the Internet.

INDEX